THE DEFINITIVE Rock 'n Roll COLLECTION
(1955 — 1966)

MW01490052

CONTENTS

HAL•LEONARD CORPORATION
7777 W. BLUEMOUND RD. P.O. BOX 13819 MILWAUKEE, WI 53213

ALL DAY AND ALL OF THE NIGHT

Words and Music by
RAY DAVIES

Trumpet

ALL SHOOK UP

Trumpet

Words and Music by OTIS BLACKWELL
and ELVIS PRESLEY

AT THE HOP

Words and Music by ARTHUR SINGER,
JOHN MADARA and DAVID WHITE

TRUMPET

(Let's go!)

BARBARA ANN

Trumpet

Words and Music by
FRED FASSERT

Bright Rock Tempo

BIG GIRLS DON'T CRY

Words and Music by BOB CREWE
and BOB GAUDIO

Trumpet

THE BIRDS AND THE BEES

Trumpet

Words and Music by
HERB NEWMAN

Moderately, with a beat

BLUE SUEDE SHOES

Words and Music by
CARL LEE PERKINS

Trumpet

Bright tempo (not too fast)

BLUE VELVET

Trumpet

Words and Music by BERNIE WAYNE
and LEE MORRIS

BLUEBERRY HILL

Words and Music by AL LEWIS,
LARRY STOCK and VINCENT ROSE

Trumpet

BOOK OF LOVE

Words & Music by WARREN DAVIS,
GEORGE MALONE and CHARLES PATRICK

Trumpet

BRISTOL STOMP

Words and Music by KAL MANN
and DAVE APPELL

Trumpet

BYE BYE, LOVE

Words and Music by FELICE BRYANT
and BOUDLEAUX BRYANT

Trumpet

Moderately fast

CALIFORNIA DREAMIN'

Words and Music by JOHN PHILLIPS
and MICHELLE PHILLIPS

Trumpet

MCA music publishing

CARA MIA

By JULIO TRAPANI
and LEE LANGE

Trumpet

Moderately

CHANTILLY LACE

Words and Music by
J.P. RICHARDSON

Trumpet

Moderate Boogie Woogie

CHAPEL OF LOVE

Words and Music by PHIL SPECTOR,
ELLIE GREENWICH and JEFF BARRY

Trumpet

COME GO WITH ME

Words and Music by
C.E. QUICK

Trumpet

DEDICATED TO THE ONE I LOVE

Words and Music by LOWMAN PAULING
and RALPH BASS

Trumpet

DO YOU WANT TO DANCE?

Words and Music by
ROBERT FREEMAN

Trumpet

Medium Rock

DON'T BE CRUEL
(TO A HEART THAT'S TRUE)

Words and Music by OTIS BLACKWELL
and ELVIS PRESLEY

Trumpet

Ad lib.

DREAM BABY (HOW LONG MUST I DREAM)

Trumpet

Words and Music by
CINDY WALKER

DREAM LOVER

Trumpet

Words and Music by
BOBBY DARIN

Moderately

DUKE OF EARL

Words and Music by EARL EDWARDS,
EUGENE DIXON and BERNICE WILLIAMS

Trumpet

EARTH ANGEL

Trumpet

Words and Music by
DOOTSIE WILLIAMS

Slowly with a beat

EIGHT DAYS A WEEK

Words and Music by JOHN LENNON
and PAUL McCARTNEY

Trumpet

Brightly, with a Swing feel

MCA music publishing

GEORGIE PORGIE

Trumpet

Words and Music by
HERB NEWMAN

GET A JOB

Words and Music by
THE SILHOUETTES

Trumpet

Moderately, with a Rockin' beat

D.S. al Coda

CODA

GLORIA

Trumpet

Words and Music by
VAN MORRISON

Steady Rock

GOOD LOVIN'

Words and Music by RUDY CLARK
and ART RESNICK

Trumpet

GREAT BALLS OF FIRE

Words and Music by OTIS BLACKWELL
and JACK HAMMER

Trumpet

HEARTBREAK HOTEL

By MAE BOREN AXTON,
TOMMY DURDEN and ELVIS PRESLEY

Trumpet

HI-HEEL SNEAKERS

Words and Music by
ROBERT HIGGENBOTHAM

Trumpet

HOUND DOG

Words and Music by JERRY LEIBER
and MIKE STOLLER

Trumpet

I GOT YOU
(I Feel Good)

Trumpet

Words and Music by
JAMES BROWN

I WANT TO HOLD YOUR HAND

Words and Music by JOHN LENNON
and PAUL McCARTNEY

Trumpet

Moderately

MCA music publishing

IF YOU WANNA BE HAPPY

Words and Music by FRANK J. GUIDA,
C. GUIDA and JOSEPH ROYSTER

Trumpet

IN THE STILL OF THE NITE
(I'll Remember)

Words and Music by
FRED PARRIS

Trumpet

IT'S MY PARTY

Words and Music by HERB WIENER,
WALLY GOLD and JOHN GLUCK, JR.

Trumpet

Moderately bright

IT'S ONLY MAKE BELIEVE

Words and Music by CONWAY TWITTY
and JACK NANCE

Trumpet

ITSY BITSY TEENIE WEENIE
YELLOW POLKADOT BIKINI

Words and Music by PAUL J. VANCE
and LEE POCKRISS

Trumpet

Brightly, with humor

JOHNNY ANGEL

Words by LYNN DUDDY
Music by LEE POCKRISS

Trumpet

Moderate tempo

JUST ONE LOOK

Words and Music by DORIS PAYNE
and GREGORY CARROLL

Trumpet

LAND OF A THOUSAND DANCES

Words and Music by CHRIS KENNER
and ANTOINE DOMINO

Trumpet

Moderately Bright Rock

To Coda ⊕

D.S. al Coda

⊕ **CODA**

Repeat and Fade

LET THE GOOD TIMES ROLL

Trumpet

Words and Music by
LEONARD LEE

Medium bounce

LET'S TWIST AGAIN

Words by KAL MANN
Music by DAVE APPELL and KAL MANN

Trumpet

Moderately

THE LION SLEEPS TONIGHT
(Wimoweh) (Mbube)

New lyric and revised music by HUGO PERETTI,
LUIGI CREATORE, GEORGE WEISS & ALBERT STANTON
Based on a song by SOLOMON LINDA and PAUL CAMPBELL

Trumpet

LOLLIPOP

Trumpet

Words and Music by BEVERLY ROSS
and JULIUS DIXON

LONG TALL SALLY

By ENOTRIS JOHNSON,
RICHARD PENNIMAN and ROBERT BLACKWELL

Trumpet

Bright Rock tempo

MCA music publishing

LOUIE, LOUIE

Words and Music by
RICHARD BERRY

Trumpet

Medium Rock beat

LOVE ME TENDER

Trumpet

Words and Music by ELVIS PRESLEY
and VERA MATSON

Moderately slow

A LOVER'S QUESTION

Words and Music by BROOK BENTON
and JIMMY WILLIAMS

Trumpet

Moderate tempo

(You've Got)
THE MAGIC TOUCH

Words and Music by
BUCK RAM

Trumpet

Moderately

MY BOYFRIEND'S BACK

Words and Music by ROBERT (BOB) FELDMAN,
GERALD (JERRY) GOLDSTEIN and RICHARD GOTTEHRER

Trumpet

MY HEART IS AN OPEN BOOK

Words by HAL DAVID
Music by LEE POCKRISS

Trumpet

Moderate slow tempo

MY PRAYER

Music by GEORGES BOULANGER
Lyric and Musical Adaptation by JIMMY KENNEDY

Trumpet

NEW ORLEANS

Words and Music by FRANK J. GUIDA
and JOSEPH F. ROYSTER

Trumpet

Moderate Rock tempo

OVER AND OVER

Words and Music by
ROBERT BYRD

Trumpet

Bright Rock tempo

PEGGY SUE

Trumpet

Words and Music by JERRY ALLISON,
NORMAN PETTY and BUDDY HOLLY

Very brightly

PIPELINE

Words and Music by BOB SPICKARD
and BRIAN CARMAN

Trumpet

PURPLE PEOPLE EATER

Trumpet

Words and Music by
SHEB WOOLEY

REBEL 'ROUSER

Words and Music by DUANE EDDY
and LEE HAZLEWOOD

Trumpet

Moderately bright

ROCK AND ROLL IS HERE TO STAY

Trumpet

Words and Music by
DAVID WHITE

ROCK AROUND THE CLOCK

By MAX C. FREEDMAN
and JIMMY DeKNIGHT

Trumpet

ROCKIN' ROBIN

Words and Music by
J. THOMAS

Trumpet

Bright Rock tempo

RUBY BABY

Trumpet

Words and Music by JERRY LEIBER
and MIKE STOLLER

RUNAWAY

Words and Music by DEL SHANNON
and MAX CROOK

Trumpet

Moderately Bright

SAVE THE LAST DANCE FOR ME

Words and Music by DOC POMUS
and MORT SHUMAN

Trumpet

SEARCHIN'

Words and Music by JERRY LEIBER
and MIKE STOLLER

Trumpet

Not too fast, with a strong afterbeat

(SEVEN LITTLE GIRLS)
SITTING IN THE BACK SEAT

Words by BOB HILLARD
Music by LEE POCKRISS

Trumpet

THE SHOOP SHOOP SONG
(IT'S IN HIS KISS)

Words and Music by
RUDY CLARK

Trumpet

SINCERELY

Words and Music by HARVEY FUQUA
and ALAN FREED

Trumpet

SOUTH STREET

Words and Music by KAL MANN
and DAVE APPELL

Trumpet

SPLISH SPLASH

Words and Music by BOBBY DARIN
and JEAN MURRAY

Trumpet

Repeat and Fade

STAND BY ME

Trumpet

Words and Music by BEN E. KING,
JERRY LEIBER and MIKE STOLLER

STAY

Words and Music by
MAURICE WILLIAMS

Trumpet

Moderately

SUGAR SHACK

Words and Music by KEITH McCORMACK
and FAYE VOSS

Trumpet

With a beat

Repeat and Fade

SUMMER IN THE CITY

Words and Music by JOHN SEBASTIAN,
STEVE BOONE and MARK SEBASTIAN

Trumpet

SUMMERTIME BLUES

Words and Music by EDDIE COCHRAN
and JERRY CAPEHART

Trumpet

THE SUNSHINE OF YOUR LOVE

Words and Music by JACK BRUCE,
PETE BROWN and ERIC CLAPTON

Trumpet

Moderate Rock

SURFER GIRL

Trumpet

Words and Music by
BRIAN WILSON

Slow Rock beat

SURFIN' U.S.A.

Music by CHUCK BERRY
Lyrics by BRIAN WILSON

Trumpet

TEARS ON MY PILLOW

Words and Music by SYLVESTOR BRADFORD
and AL LEWIS

Trumpet

Moderate 12/8 feel

THAT'LL BE THE DAY

Words and Music by JERRY ALLISON,
NORMAN PETTY and BUDDY HOLLY

Trumpet

THE TWIST

Words and Music by
HANK BALLARD

Trumpet

UNDER THE BOARDWALK

Words and Music by ARTIE RESNICK
and KENNY YOUNG

Trumpet

VENUS

Words and Music by
EDWARD MARSHALL

Trumpet

MCA music publishing

WAKE UP, LITTLE SUSIE

Words and Music by BOUDLEAUX BRYANT
and FELICE BRYANT

Trumpet

WALK AWAY RENEE

Words and Music by MIKE BROWN,
TONY SANSONE and BOB CALILLI

Trumpet

WHOLE LOTTA SHAKIN' GOIN' ON

Words and Music by SUNNY DAVID
and DAVID WILLIAMS

Trumpet

Moderately, with a solid beat

WILD THING

Words and Music by
CHIP TAYLOR

WILLIE AND THE HAND JIVE

Words and Music by
JOHNNY OTIS

Trumpet

WOOLY BULLY

Trumpet

Words and Music by
DOMINGO SAMUDIO

Moderately

YAKETY YAK

Words and Music by JERRY LEIBER
and MIKE STOLLER

Trumpet

Bright tempo

(Spoken) Don't talk back.

(Spoken) Don't talk back.

(Spoken) Don't talk back.

YOU REALLY GOT ME

Words and Music by
RAY DAVIES

Trumpet

YOU TURN ME ON

Words and Music by
IAN WHITCOMB

Trumpet

Bright Rock beat